Under the Influence

MONTANA *Estates*

Essay Series

Other titles by Bill Manhire

SONGS OF MY LIFE, 1996 *(short fiction)*

WHAT TO CALL YOUR CHILD, 1999 *(poems)*

DOUBTFUL SOUNDS : ESSAYS AND INTERVIEWS, 2000

COLLECTED POEMS, 2001

Under the Influence

Bill Manhire

Series editor: Lloyd Jones

FOUR
WINDS
PRESS

Four Winds Press
Wellington

© Bill Manhire 2003

ISBN 0-9582375-6-5

First published September 2003

Airplane Studios
Typeset in Perpetua

Printed by Printlink

I left my baby lying here,
Lying here, lying here;
I left my baby lying here
To go and gather blaeberries.

That was my mother's song. She sang it to me and my baby brother. There was sadness for Scotland in it, and perhaps for other things. Before I went to school I had her Scottish accent. The song was a lullaby and it helped us fall asleep.

Rovan, govan, gorry-a-go,
Gorry-a-go, gorry-a-go,
Rovan, govan gorry-a-go,
I never found my baby-oh …

My mother, Maisie, came from Edinburgh. Her parents had eloped from Northern Ireland (poor and wealthy families), and her father, who had been born to the wealthy family, worked as a railway signalman through the rest of his life. He changed the points on the Edinburgh–Kings Cross line, and made the great trains switch from track to track.

When I was little, I wrote to him, and he sent me back an air letter. It was dated 19th Oct, 1951, and addressed to Master Bill Manhire, Wallacetown Hotel, Invercargill, Southland, New Zealand:

Dear Bill

Thank you for your nice letter.

I expect you will soon be going to School now, and then you will be able to write us long letters and tell us more.

The boys and girls here are all back at School after their Summer holiday. The boys played Cricket during the summer. In winter they play Association Football & Rugger.

We would like very much to see you. But it isn't likely we will ever go to New Zealand. So

you must come to see us, & bring Ian with you &
see the beautiful City of Edinburgh where we live.
You have Uncles and Aunts & many cousins here.
I'm sure they would all be pleased to see you. Ask
your mother to tell you about them sometime. Tell
your mother we are just getting along in our old
usual way. We had a poor Summer but a very fine
Autumn. Now we are rather dreading the Winter
when it can be very cold here.

We hope you will write us again.

Love to you & Ian

from
Granma & Granddad Aitken

Maisie was a scholarship girl who went to Mary
Erskine School for Girls (Miss Jean Brodie territory), then took a science degree at Edinburgh
University and became a high-school teacher. Like
her sisters, she was probably destined for a life of
middle-class spinsterhood (their mother, a "hard"
woman, discouraged marriage where her sons and

daughters were concerned, and refused to attend any of their weddings).

Then, during the war, Maisie met a New Zealand sailor. I suppose that, more than usual, she and Jack rescued one another from the lives they might have led. He was 34, she 30. Marriage for Maisie meant New Zealand, the far side of the world. Yet while she lost her family – her hard mother and loving father, her brothers and her sisters – she also escaped from a world of grey severities, where a kind of dour disapproval can rebuke even the happiest events.

When my daughter Vanessa was born in 1973, I rang my Aunt Margaret in Edinburgh: "Hello, Aunt Margaret. Great news! We've had a baby!"

"And what is it?"

"Well, it's a girl, Aunt Margaret."

"Och well, never mind."

"But that's fine, Aunt Margaret. We're very happy, and anyway, you know, we'll just make sure and have a boy next time so as to balance things up."

A lengthy Scottish pause.

"I wouldn't count on that if I were you."

My mother sailed into Wellington Harbour on St Valentine's Day 1946, on a ship full of war brides. My father met her and they drove down to Dunedin. Somewhere halfway down the West Coast, it crossed her mind that they could just drive and drive for ever yet never get to Scotland. She remembers Jack taking her to a Dunedin pub after hours, and that one of the drinkers spat into a fireplace, and how the gob flamed up because it was, as someone there explained to her, pure spirit. She had married a man who liked a drink.

They moved to Invercargill, where all the streets were named after Scottish rivers. On 4 November 1946, the first purpose-built hotel run by the newly established Invercargill Licensing Trust, the Southland, opened for business. Above the entrance to the bar were the words: "Jack Manhire – Licensed to sell fermented and spirituous liquors".

*

Southland, Green Roofs, Railway, Oak Tree Inn, Crown, St Kilda – they are somehow the same place. For example, each one was full of drunk people.

I was born in the Southland Hotel, two days after Christmas 1946. My earliest memory is being chased up some stairs by some bigger children.

*

My father must always have wanted to be in pubs. I have some notes he made for his mother as he travelled across America en route to the United Kingdom.

After a meal a Yank sailor did his best to show us the town. In Frisco every restaurant is a pub & every pub a restaurant & in addition hundreds of odd grocers sell spirits by the bottle. After having a few drinks in the city we took a taxi to Chinatown & had a good look around – Spent a good deal of time in a nightclub called "The Lion's Den" where they have "Floor Shows" & a bar in the one room. There are dozens of these places, no charge being made to go in but they charge about five dollars for five or six drinks & you have to tip them on top of that, so you will realise it costs you something to get out of the place. From Chinatown we walked a short distance to the International Settlement (which incidentally is the old Barbary Coast) & finished up at a big Night Club called the "International Club". This club is apparently run by negroes for their own crowd & five of us were the only whites among hundreds of niggers. However they did not seem to object & we stopped for about an hour listening to some really hot music & stage shows & had a few more Dewars or Black Labels. By this time it was midnight & as all bars & shows (with the exception of picture theatres

15

which go until 5 AM) close at 12 o'clock we started to wander back. We called at a restaurant & had a steak which cost us 2 dollars 20 cents the equivalent of about 14/- NZ Currency & then home to bed.

Jack was on his way to England to train as a naval officer. A friend from Lancing College where they were training as officer cadets early in 1944 told me that he had a nickname, "Count" – "because he had the uncanny knack of not only being senior in age but also making our money go further, by visiting the dog races whenever we had a chance. I can recall that we spent a few days in Edinburgh together and your Father had an introduction to Distillers Limited. We were shown around the distillery and given a sample of their wares in the form of a flask of George Four – this enabled us to sleep well on the return to Hove."

In fact, he could bed down anywhere, an aunt once told me: "All that sleeping on the decks."

*

Prohibition came to Invercargill early last century. In June 1906, there were 16 hotels for a population of 13,000; in July, none. However, there had been a legal hiccup. While retail liquor outlets were obliged to close, the two local breweries fell outside the new legislation. They not only continued in business but also sold their beer through hotels beyond the town boundary. They even set up their own sales depots: one side of the street was dry; on the other, the citizens of Invercargill went on buying their bottles, jars and kegs.

On election night 1943 the votes of Second World War servicemen produced a restoration majority. The Invercargill Licensing Trust opened its first bars in converted buildings nearly a year later. One of the biggest early arguments had been over whether drinkers should be able to stand or sit. The Trust chairman fought successfully for the standing option on the grounds that only "sissies and primps" sit down to drink. But the *Southland Times* had pronounced the Trust to be "the most important

17

experiment ever tried in the conduct and control of the liquor trade in New Zealand", and so it would need to respect the current laws and protocols. Six o'clock closing had been in force nationally since 1916. In Invercargill, it meant what it said: *Time gentlemen, please.*

Beyond the city boundaries, in the old wet areas, after-hours trading flourished. The Green Roofs hotel at Wallacetown, where we moved in 1949, was one of those beyond the boundary. One week, the court news in the *Southland Times* recorded the convictions of three of our customers driving back into Invercargill. One was drunk in charge of a motor vehicle, one drunk in charge of a bicycle, the third drunk in charge of a horse-and-cart.

Counterlunch was one of the ways in which pubs competed. Free food was served into the bar at exactly 5 p.m., the timing no doubt designed to encourage regulars to start drinking well before closing time. The Makarewa freezing works was just down the road, so that alongside the standard fare of saveloys, sausages and toasted cheese (the spread was a mixture of cheese, onions and stout), the Green Roofs was the recipient of cases of kidneys and sweetbreads.

*

Someone made a home movie in 1952. It doesn't show counterlunch or the dirty Makarewa River which ran behind the pub, where sugarbags full of drowned kittens bumped quietly on the bottom. It doesn't show the way reins fall on a horse's neck, or how at the races the men stood around the boots of their cars, pouring drinks and consulting racebooks. It doesn't show Jack driving an inebriated farmer home in the farmer's car while Maisie followed behind in ours. There is nothing about Rumpelstiltskin or Mowgli the jungle boy or the dog with eyes like saucers.

The film starts with my first day at school. I am wearing my maroon blazer – the Southland colours – and I march out the front door of the Green

Roofs, advancing towards the camera with my leather satchel, till my mother turns me in the right direction. Seconds later I am sitting at the end of a six-seater desk, staring at an inkwell. Wallacetown school was famous at the time for the fact that its teaching staff was 100 percent All Blacks. The headmaster, Tubby Holden, had once played halfback for New Zealand. His assistant, Bill McCaw, was a current loose forward; he taught me my multiplication tables.

There are other things: some white swans, and a wandering peacock; roses and ponds with lily pads – which must mean Queen's Gardens. My brother Ian and I are on swings. My mother and father love him more but this is because he is so little. Then we are at the beach – Riverton, where the racecourse is painted orange – and shivering as we come out of the water into a blue-grey world. Suddenly I recall my mishearing of my mother's word for the biscuits she gave us as we dried off: *shivery bites*. There are shots of me doing somersaults, mainly to indicate that my little brother – who is busy copying me –

can't manage this astonishing activity. Then we are both sitting on the grass pretending to read books, holding them out to the camera. And there are picnic shots: my mother eating a sandwich (how young she is!), two other young women linking arms and giggling. And my father, just a glimpse really, ducking out of the shot, holding his hat across his face. In the film he is much younger than I am now, but as he flees from the frame he still looks older. Somehow he will always know best. It's like the woman who was shown in the paper the other day, celebrating her 102nd birthday with her 82-year-old daughter and 69-year-old son. There they are in a Masterton rest home, decked out in party hats. The story says that Winnie Miller is still telling her children what to do. "I really have to growl sometimes. The kids need to know right from wrong."

*

Nor does the film show *Manhire Concrete Posts and Strainers*. These days, if you leave Wallacetown in the direction of Riverton, then the second-last house on your right is where we lived after we left the Green Roofs. It was a proper house, so for a while we must have been a proper family. Just past it is a mouldering section whose frontage is a fence with high, ancient, weathered concrete posts. At one time they were clean and new, advertising their own capacities. There are still holes in the posts for wires. Behind is a sort of building, a tumble-down shed, really. This was the heart of my father's short-lived industrial kingdom: Manhire Concrete Posts and Strainers. In the early 1950s, pastoral New Zealand was full of post-war paddocks waiting to be fenced or re-fenced. But the new-fangled concrete posts and strainers probably needed to be manufactured by someone other than a man who employed two others to do the work while he went off to the pub or the races. I remember, a couple of years later, sitting in the front passenger seat of our pale blue Vauxhall Velox as he drove down to Invercargill from Mossburn. Something had gone wrong with Manhire Concrete Posts and Strainers, and the car was going to be sold when we got there. But there must still be a scatter of farms across Southland where the Manhire fenceposts go on taking the strain.

*

Maisie had hoped to go back to school teaching, maybe at Southland Girls' High. One night she and Jack sat up the whole of the night arguing; and after that we moved to Mossburn and another pub. Between schools I somehow skipped a year and went straight into Standard One. (It is not a good thing to be a year younger than your classmates: I was out of my depth for ever.)

The Mossburn Hotel had been established in 1886 by the appropriately named George Beer, who moved a building from Castle Rock to be adjacent to the spot where the rumoured branch railway line from Lumsden would likely fetch up. He called the pub the Railway, and by the time we arrived it was a two-storey brick building, with a little private garden to one side. This is the garden where I taught myself to fly. The sensation of flying is my strongest childhood memory. There was nothing transcendental about it, just my clumsy, dogged, learner's breaststroke as I dreamed my way round and round the safe, enclosed space of the garden, pulling myself through the heavy air, a steady three feet above the earth. It was sheer effort gave me the necessary lift, though it never took me high enough to see the paddocks and stables behind the hotel, where we had a few cows (and our own cream churn), some sheep, muscovy ducks and hens. There were also some baby pigs brought in by hunters.

There was another kind of flying in Mossburn. Bill Hewitt, one of the legendary characters of the infant topdressing industry, was based there. He pushed the law to the limit in all sorts of ways. There's a story about a Customs official hiring him to fly over the Hokonui Hills in search of illegal whiskey stills, and how the plane from time to time encountered unexpected turbulence. One of his planes was the Miles Aerovan, a dumpy, twin-engined lump of a thing, just a tin belly, really. Bill Hewitt used it to ferry construction materials and workers during the building of the Roxburgh hydrodam, though his cargoes also included whitebait, live cattle and, once, a tractor.

On 31 January 1954, we clambered into the Aerovan and flew over Milford Sound to stare far down to where the *Gothic* and her escort the *Black Prince* lay in the inky blue water. The Queen was making a scenic detour on her departure from New Zealand. I remember that the Aerovan was unpainted, inside and out, and that we sat along the sides. It crashed just under a month later. There were misty conditions on a job near Roxburgh, and Bill Hewitt flew round and round in search of clear sky until he ran out of petrol – at which point he made an emergency landing in a turnip paddock next to the Ranfurly airstrip. The pilot walked away from the wreck, but the plane was a write-off.

In fact, there was plenty of seeding and topdressing work locally: the area was famed for what it could do with grass seed. "The splendid farming community of Mossburn is a modest, prudently run district with a world-wide significance far out of proportion to its size," pronounced the *New Zealand Freelance*. "There is the virtual home of the purple-headed grass that in half a century has won global acclaim – Chewings fescue." Chewings fescue – also known as "N.Z. Hard" – produced strong, hard-wearing surfaces. The courts at Wimbledon were grassed with it; so was the pitch at Lords. During the war, fescue grown from Mossburn seed was used for temporary airstrips right across Britain. There must have been a kind of grass-seed fever throughout the district, for the local kids used to work as cocksfooters, ferociously beating out seed from grasses gathered from the roadside or along the railway line. We used tarpaulins from the railway wagons. But this was the trivial world of pocket money. The farmers round Mossburn were seriously wealthy; people called them the Fescue Kings.

Mossburn was also on the way through to the lakes. To the west were Manapouri and Te Anau; north was Wakatipu — the deep, black Kingston end of the lake. So there were tourists in the summer, catered to by the hotel and by a brand-new, bright blue milk bar. There were several churches, but no resident ministers. There was also a general store which sold lollies and comics, and sometimes films were screened by the school committee in the local hall. For a while Miss Haversham woke me each night, screaming as she burned to death amid the cobwebs of her cake and bridal dress. In the summer heat we played in dense jungles of crackling broom beside the railway line, and sometimes hitched a ride on a hand jigger. In the winter, the snow might drift to the tops of the picket fences. We made sledges. Every snowflake was different. There was ice on the insides of windows.

Ted, the Railway's cowman-gardener, could stand on his head and drink a glass of beer, and would generally do so if someone bought the beer for him. Lonely men appeared out of the bush from time to time, stayed a few nights, then vanished. One deerstalker had been a Maori All Black; he would unpack his kit and ask Maisie to iron his football jersey. There were rabbiters, shearers, hunters, casual farmhands – and commercial travellers whose cases were lined with shining jewellery and watches.

*

In Mossburn Jack had opened a second branch of Manhire Concrete Posts and Strainers. He had a partner, says Maisie, but he diddled him. Is this when Jack went bankrupt? Did he even go bankrupt at all? Maisie doesn't think so, but then, "He never really told me anything."

But just as there was a moment when we drove all the way to Invercargill to sell the car, there was also a time when we were no longer in the hotel, but instead were living in Mick Cournane's old abandoned farmhouse because after he and his family had moved into their brand-new one they were doing the decent thing and helping us out. Mick was Catholic but his wife was a Jehovah's

Witness. This was baffling because everyone knew that if the Jehovah's Witnesses knocked on your door, you just had to say you were Catholic and they would be off like a shot. Their daughter, Jewel, used to carry copies of *The Watchtower* in her schoolbag. At Mossburn school we learnt about clouds — *cirrus, cumulus, cumulonimbus* — and later, as we walked back across the paddocks from the school bus, Jewel explained how after death she would be saved and live in Paradise on earth. She would stroll among peaceful golden lions. But I was doomed for ever.

Outside the old Cournane place I kicked a football to and fro beneath the pines which darkened the air around the house. Our hut was up there in one of them: planks with a sway. At night I lay in bed and worried about the escaped prisoners. It said about them on the radio. Sometimes they hid in the bush and broke into people's houses to drink the grog. Even now one might be making his way across the paddocks, creeping from one windbreak to the next. What if he spotted our farmhouse? Our mother always left the back door unlocked so our father could let himself in when he came back late at night. What if a prisoner was watching our house from under the pines? Where was our father?

It turned out that we were waiting for our Wallacetown house to come free, and soon we were back there for a while. Wallacetown school had lost its All Blacks, and Maisie quarreled with the new teacher, so each day we took the bus to Waikiwi school on the outskirts of Invercargill. All I remember about Waikiwi is that I fell in love – aged eight, and from a speechless distance – with a pair of identical twins, a problem solved when we moved once again. We were leaving Southland and going north to Otago.

*

These days Clinton seems trapped midway on the main road between Gore and Balclutha, one of the few places in the south to have missed the rural recovery. In the fifties it was a rich farming settlement and railway town, nestled under Popotunoa, a big hill which in milder landscapes might have been a mountain. Passenger trains and the railcar stopped several times a day at the long station platform because of the Railway Refreshment Rooms. There were two grocery stores, a draper's, a milk bar, a garage, a post office and the RSA, as well as a brand-new Coronation Hall, constructed entirely of corrugated iron. Perhaps Clinton's greatest claim to fame was the long, narrow swimming pool, which locals claimed was the longest open-air pool in the Southern Hemisphere. It was fed by the Kuriwao stream: water was piped in one end and out the other. Sometimes you couldn't see to the bottom. If the filtering system broke you might find small fish in there. Once I saw a man sit on the side, unstrap his wooden leg and then just topple in.

The Oak Tree Inn was brand new, one of the first pubs opened by the Clutha Licensing Trust. There was a real oak tree; Jack's name was there above the door; and on opening day he turned on free beer. A cartoon in one of the Dunedin papers shows men happily strolling out of the pub, laden with kegs and bottles, and staring indignantly at a car with an Auckland number plate: "Now I call that REALLY over the edge!"

"Jack Manhire," said the publican in Tuatapere a couple of years ago. "That name would still mean quite a bit round here." I tend to recall my father as a weak, lost soul, someone who drank away his gifts and income on the wrong side of the bar, but the memory must be for my own convenience, for in his heyday he was clearly someone of charm and capacity. When I stopped in Clinton recently I was reminded once again. "He gave this place a lift with all his life and energy and fresh ideas," Rona Barnett told me. "You know, he organised some big banquets. They loved him at the RSA. I remember once he got the Tin Hat Club down from Dunedin. More loaves of bread than you've ever seen! Ducks! Geese, even! I've never known so much food. It was a banquet, a feast."

*

The past seems empty until you turn and stare at it. I find myself short of sequence and narrative – the *and then* of my own life defeats me – but the clutter of moments is everywhere. I am on top of a ladder on a back road, out for the day with the Post and Telegraph crew; they are staying at the pub and putting in new phone lines all over South Otago; the porcelain things on the poles are called cups. I am fishing in the Pomahaka River, or watching an eel someone has caught slither off across a paddock. I am being a lead dog, walking along a dusty road somewhere up the Kuriwao Gorge; behind me there is a flock of sheep and the yapping of real dogs; this is not entirely dignified, yet how amazing that you can just walk quietly in the sun and all the sheep will follow! I am making winter mash for the hens, or chopping kindling from pale white whiskey boxes: *Bell's Afore Ye Go!* At school we are taken outside to watch a jet plane fly over because we have finally broken the sound barrier. Late at night a train shunts across the road just past my bedroom window. I have a Davy Crockett hat. It is actually made out of possums.

And at the Coronation Hall there were the flicks: *Reach for the Sky, The Dam Busters, Tammy*. But films were strange: you couldn't go inside them. Anyway, I was lost in books and comics: Enid Blyton, the *William* stories, *Batman and Robin*, *Superman*, *Plasticman* (he could turn himself into a table lamp or reach beneath a door to wrap his hand around a villain's throat). I cut out *The Phantom* and *Mandrake the Magician* from the newspaper and pasted them into scrapbooks; at school I wrote my *Tarzan* and *Biggles* serials. Each week my mother went to the Gore library and brought me back a bag of books. I even started my own library, a remarkable community scheme whereby my friends gave me all their books to keep at the Oak Tree Inn and I issued them back on loan. At Christmas *Oor Wullie* albums were sent from Scotland. One cover showed him sitting on his upturned bucket reading the same comic album I was holding, and there on its cover was a smaller version of Oor Wullie reading the same comic album, and so on and so on and so on, repeating for ever out into the universe … How could anyone see that far?

I was thought to be musical. I learned to play the chanter with the Clinton Pipe Band, and was sent for proper music lessons to Miss Bunbury. I stood beside her drawing-room piano and sang the songs of Stephen Foster:

> Thou wilt come no more, gentle Annie,
> Like a flower thy spirit did depart;
> Thou art gone, alas! like the many
> That have bloomed in the summer of my heart.

Sometimes I was hauled out of bed late at night and led through to the bar to sing the "Invercargill March" ...

> In-ver-car-gill, tis
> the only place that I adore ...

And then my mother would sing Jack's favourite song, while he held his glass of whiskey and looked solemn:

I know where I'm going,
and I know who's going with me;
I know who I love,
but the dear knows who I'll marry.

Some say he's black,
but I say he's bonny;
fairest of them all
is my handsome, winsome, Johnny.

We went for Sunday drives. My father gestured at shops: "That place could be a little gold mine." Sometimes we drove to Kaka Point, or into the Catlins where we stopped at little sawmills deep in the bush. More often, we pulled up outside a pub somewhere. "I'll only be a couple of ticks," Jack would say or, more mysteriously, "Just going to see a man about a dog." Then we would be left in the car to wait for him. Once, the Trust got in a relief manager and we went for a holiday at Karitane, north of Dunedin. After we had been on the road for ten minutes, Jack told Maisie that earlier that morning there had been a phone call from Scotland:

her mother was dead.

At the end of 1958 I turned 12, and the next year started high school 20 miles away in Balclutha. Each day on the bus I was bullied. A few of the bigger kids spent the 50-minute journey slapping the legs of the Third Formers. You sat there and endured it, slap, because if you fought back or cried or complained to a teacher, much worse would happen. Slap. I wish I could remember their names and take the entirely magical revenge of words on a page. The two worst bullies were brothers whose parents ran the Clinton milk bar. On the way back, they didn't bother. Somehow it was the prospect of the day ahead that made them what they were.

Then we were on the move again, this time to the Crown Hotel, 179 Rattray Street, Dunedin. Jack had the chance of a lease and could organise the money. He and Maisie and Ian shifted north in the middle of the year, but it had been decided that my schooling should not be interrupted, and that I would board in Clinton with the local stock-and-station agent. Russell was a bachelor, and he had a *fiancée*. This meant they were engaged to be married. Sometimes at night the house would be empty, all dark wood and carpet. Russell and his fiancée were out in the back-yard caravan. I had just bought my first pop record, "Lipstick On Your Collar": I knew what they were doing.

*

Someone must have stood on a chair behind the bar to take the photograph. My mother thinks it is 1963 and that all the police are staying in the hotel because of the Royal visit. It is certainly the public bar of the Crown, though none of the public are there, only 24 policemen, not quite in uniform but not quite out of it either. They all wear sportscoats over shirts and ties. Most of them have a glass in one hand, a cigarette in the other, and are looking up at the camera. The two figures not holding drinks are my father, Jack, and the most senior-looking policeman. Jack has that well-oiled, late-in-the-day expression – glazed eyes and a silly smile. His right arm is linked through the policeman's left arm. They are like a bridal couple, except that the groom already resembles a long-suffering middle-aged husband and the bride seems to be drunk at her own wedding.

The prohibitionists were right: throughout New Zealand there was a kind of *de facto* marriage between the hotel trade and the police. Six o'clock closing had been brought in as a temporary measure during the First World War and had somehow never been got rid of. It was simply the most bizarre of many strange compromises between the liquor industry and the forces of temperance. The effect was that the consumption of alcohol became divorced from other social and community activities. Even legal drinking took place out of sight, behind frosted windows. You could hear the dangerous noises, the shameful hubbub, from the street, and sometimes the human evidence would lurch out through the door. New Zealand must be the only country in the world which has a dictionary entry for "six o'clock swill".

Yet there was something sad when in 1967 six o'clock closing was abolished. With it went a kind of wonderful uproar, a thundering, male exuberance (not to mention counterlunch), and the easy understanding between police and publicans began to dissolve. For, really, things were once so civilised. At the St Kilda, which Jack and Maisie ran after the Crown, the local South Dunedin police would usually pay a visit at 6.30 p.m. to make sure the bars were cleared, and sometimes they would call again at 10.30 p.m. For the hours in between, however, it was business as usual. Once or twice a year, just for the books, they called at nine o'clock, but there was always a preliminary phone message – "Might be down your way in ten minutes, Jack" – and the drinkers would nick quickly out the back door or, if they were still keen to make an evening of it, would stand out in the yard till, 20 minutes later, the premises had been inspected and pronounced empty.

Hotels made a lot of their money after hours, and at the Crown the after-hours trade was serious

business. A bar had to be open, anyway, for regis-
tered guests, and anyone could legally drink there
as long as they were being entertained by a guest.
Customers gave three short rings, taxis four; but
a police visit was signalled by a single long ring.
In the infinitely stretched interval between that
sustained ring on the bell and the answering of the
door, drinkers were hastily assigned to hotel guests;
and sometimes, if things were very busy, it might
be necessary to call down to the bar the hotel's
three or four permanent boarders. The perms were
solitary men whose cut-price accommodation was
guaranteed by their willingness to "cover" drinkers
after hours. Once every three or four weeks a perm
boarder might find himself trying to remember
the names of half a dozen inebriated strangers, or
assuring an officer of the law that, yes, he certainly
was paying for all the drinks.

*

A few years later, when we were in the St Kilda
Hotel, I was woken at about two in the morn-

ing by the sound of car doors slamming down in the street. Then the doorbell rang and men were yelling at one another, and I heard a clanging as someone started to clamber up the fire escape. Then my window was being hoisted open, and a policeman was standing over my bed.

"Where's the boss? Tell him to open up!"

He was a sergeant, in his early 30s, very drunk, with the build and colouring of a Springbok loose forward. Jack got out of bed, not yet quite sober himself, and opened up the back bar for the sergeant and his two off-siders. We listened at the top of the stairs while for several hours they drank on the house. Eventually, they all passed out, and Jack phoned the Dunedin central police station. Just before daylight, men from the morning watch came and took the whole of that night's duty watch away.

"No-hopers," said one of the barmen next day. "Wouldn't have happened with six o'clock closing."

*

"Your dad cleaned this place up," customers at the Crown liked to tell me. Even old Tip, who drank in the front bar in the mornings and had once ridden on a horse-drawn cart beneath a sign that said *Strike out the top line!*, reckoned it was so. "Yes, this place was a dump, mainly ratbags till your father came along." And he would tip his hat expressively in the direction of McLaggan Street, up which there were three pubs somehow still letting the side down. In fact, Jack made the Crown safe for commercial travellers and race-horse owners, and the monthly meetings of the Brevet Club. He always wore a suit. After a while, he stopped going behind the bar. Instead, he played "mine host", drinking with his customers, moving from group to group, shouting his round. The customers were mostly middle-class men who played cards and bet on horses, and grumbled about the way the world was going. Maisie tells me that Gerry Merito came into the Crown one night after hours. Presumably the Howard Morrison Quartet had just finished a show in town. He looked around at the bar full of euchre-playing, inebriated men in suits, uttered the one word, "Squaresville!", and went somewhere more interesting.

Jack's loyal customers were entirely loyal to him. Ralph Hotere told me recently that he had been to the funeral of one of our old customers, Allen Percival. "Your dad was mentioned." One of the speakers had made a point of saying how Allen "had followed Jack Manhire from the Crown to the St Kilda". Some people follow their spiritual advisors in much the same way. And like any preacher or entertainer, Jack had his signature phrases – especially a few ritual calls designed to clear the bar. I don't think I ever heard him say, "Time gentlemen, please", or "Last orders". But I still have in my head as resonant noises the Irish farewell (courtesy of First Corinthians), "Have you no homes?", the Churchillian "Our finest hour!", and – obscure of origin yet best of all – "Home, little bastards, home!"

*

I remember hearing James K. Baxter deliver a lecture on his poem "Henley Pub" at Otago University. The poem is spoken by an alcoholic commercial traveller:

> ... The barman's heel
> Crushes a hot butt, and I
> Burn. The vacillations of the sky
> Shine through the brandy glass ...

"The barman," explained Baxter, "is a symbol of the natural order which is now rejecting him [the speaker]. His life still contains the heat of pain and desire; it is burnt down, though, like the cigarette butt. To an alcoholic a barman may seem at times almost almighty, the dispenser of life and death; and the crushing of the butt could even be an image of his possible extinction under the heel of God."

This is splendid waffle. True, the barman stands higher than his customers, reflected in the mirrors which also multiply the glasses and bottles behind him. But his job is to sell alcohol. In all the jokes, the barman serves and suffers fools gladly. *A duck walked into a bar. "What'll it be?" said the barman.* In some essential way he is a piece of amiable false-ness. He adjusts his point of view to his customer's – listening, grunting, agreeing, prompting with a question – or he disagrees within a safe territory, like tomorrow's weather. No politics, no religion, is the old adage. At the end of the Baxter poem, after the commercial traveller's pronouncement that

> that is all;
> All; Jehovah's sky
> And earth like millstones grind us small.

a real barman would probably have grunted and said, "Yes, you can put a ring round that."

Of course the barman does have power. At the St Kilda Hotel there was a pensioner called Henry who used to come into the bar in the mornings.

He lived in a shed in someone's small back yard, and a rich smell always kept him company. The bar staff liked Henry, and wanted to let him have a drink, but they had to keep the comfort of other customers in mind. So before he was served, Henry would wait patiently until he had been sprayed with air freshener. He would raise his arms like a child hoping to be lifted. Sometimes he smelt of lemons, sometimes of roses.

I started serving behind the bar occasionally after hours at the Crown, and by the time we were at the St Kilda I found myself working quite hard. The aim was to pour beer as fast as possible. The hose-gun was a piece of apparatus inspired by six o'clock closing – essentially a trigger attached to a long, trailing line which enabled you to rove at will, filling glasses wherever they were placed for service. Sometimes customers reached across the first rank of drinkers, so that you could even fill a jug in mid-air. I still have the remains of a callus on the second joint of my right forefinger where I held the hose-gun and squeezed. Pubs at the time were giant plumbing systems. Beer tankers – another late-fifties New Zealand innovation – discharged their contents by hose into cellar tanks; the barman used another hose to fill the glasses. A.R.D. Fairburn once suggested that drinkers could simply be dispensed with, and the bar hoses connected straight through to the men's urinal.

In the mid-1960s the Licensing Control Commission moved through New Zealand's hotels on a mission to improve accommodation standards ahead of the frequently predicted tourist boom. In the process, many of New Zealand's small country pubs were destroyed by the requirement that they offer almost the same accommodation standards as city hotels. The LCC also reallocated a restricted number of licences where it thought demand existed: hence the Once-Were-Warriors booze-barns of the seventies and eighties. We can probably also blame them for the ways in which New Zealand hotels refurbished themselves in chrome and formica, bizarre leaner bars, and roaring technicolor carpets. In Dunedin, the Commission managed to offend the whole drinking population by attacking the design and décor of the city's small pubs. They spoke sarcastically of the city's "old harridans", and sprinkled adjectives like *pitiful* and *dreary* through their report. The Crown got the standard chrome-and-formica treatment, while among specifically required alterations were such things as: "Old panelled ceiling to front entrance and vestibule to be replaced and concealed by a false ceiling." The Crown was a three-storey brick and plaster building erected in 1861. Its panelled ceiling might have been worth hanging on to.

*

Once a friend of Jack's from Wellington came to stay at the Crown. He was ex-Air Force, and was on a trip to take scenic photographs for the Government Tourist Bureau: Milford Sound, Lake Mathieson. He was also an amateur magician. He could pluck a smoking cigarette out of thin air. When I declared that I, too, aspired to be a magician, he took me round the corner to the big

Whitcombe & Tombs in Princes Street.

"What you need is a decent book about sleight of hand."

He found one quickly, Jean Hugard and Frederick Braue's *Expert Card Technique*. It was one of the classics of card conjuring, and explained in detail the dark arts of palming, bottom dealing, false cuts.

"But this is ridiculously expensive!" he said, and went over to the counter. "I wonder if I might borrow a pencil and a rubber?"

There was no rubber, but he decided the pencil would do. We went back over to the shelving on the far wall, and there in broad daylight he crossed out 51/6 and wrote beneath it 41/6. We then walked back over to the counter.

"Thank you so very much," he said to the girl, and passed across the pencil. "And while I'm here, I'll have this."

What nonchalance! I was beside myself with happiness as the tale went round the bar. Jack was aghast. Some great rule of human decency had been betrayed. Later that night, after the shops closed, he put a ten-shilling note in a manila envelope and slid it under the bookshop door.

"Doing the decent thing" was one of his favourite phrases. He was indignant with men who didn't stand their round or pay their debts: they were no longer part of a moral universe. He talked about the golden rule. At night he would sit on the end of my bed and drunkenly confide that everything he had ever done was "for you kids and your mother". A soft self-pity was on his breath like whiskey. Then he would stumble off to his own bed as if he had managed to solve something.

His desire to do the decent thing was hardly separable from a need to be liked. In practice, the decent thing meant an extravagant generosity directed at everyone except his own family. He liked being the one who shouted. I remember, aged nine or ten, being outraged when he gave a ten-shilling note to some kids we had never met before who were visiting Clinton; they immediately spent their small fortune on ice creams and giant bags of lollies. Jack was trying to indicate something to their parents. But five or six years later, at the Crown, I was outraged in a wiser way when one of his drinking circle, Doug Green, made a sly sexual overture to me. I complained to my parents. My father took Doug Green's side and told me not to be silly. Somehow I had made a mistake; my behaviour was letting everyone down.

Was that the time I refused to speak with him for months on end? Or was the aggressive, self-regarding silence I cultivated prompted by something more trivial, like a hypocritical homily after he caught me smoking? I remember enjoying my own cold triumph as we passed in the corridor or on the stairs, I suppose because I knew it bewildered him. Early in the day he gave as good as he got; late at night it was another story. But I knew I could outlast him.

Was I ever frightened by drunk people? asks my wife. But I don't think so: they were there from the beginning, they were normal. Adults were taller: they also swayed and staggered, or burst into unexpected song. I do remember a drunk man being led down the corridor at the Crown – it was a gentlemanly, civilised eviction – and how he turned suddenly and smashed a bottle of whiskey over my father's head. The event had none of the excitement of a cowboy movie. The bottle was wrapped in a brown paper bag. My father passed out, while Lofty – Lofty who? (he had been a wrestler once, but it wasn't Lofty Blomfield) – knocked the assailant to the ground, then sat on him.

It never occurred to Jack or his friends and customers that any of them might be alcoholics. That is probably why the face which stared from the Crown's flagon label never bothered anyone. It belonged to someone who might have stepped off a Mississippi riverboat: a lopsided moustache, large ears, and a spectacularly red nose separating a double set of bloodshot eyes. On his spotted yellow shirt were the words:

Drinking again, eh?
PRESSURE BEER
from
CROWN HOTEL DUNEDIN

No one who drank at the Crown looked like that and, anyway, alcoholics were other people (or, as Dylan Thomas once put it, people you don't like who drink as much as you do). Real alkies were loners who drank at home and kept flagons of cheap sherry or port under the bed. A man had to be able to hold his drink, of course; but then, he had to be able to drink a lot in the first place to show he could do so. Occasionally someone you knew ended up in Cherry Farm, being dried out. That was serious. But if you went to hospital for some physical sickness, your friends smuggled in cigarettes and whiskey. It was all a great joke. Cheers, everyone said. Good health.

As time went on Jack drank more and more. For him, working in the bar meant drinking in the bar, and a day that started with a drink or two with a customer at lunchtime might not end until midnight. In his last few years, I would guess he was drinking perhaps a couple of bottles of whiskey a day. And at one point it wasn't a great joke. He was in hospital, cirrhosis of the liver, and the doctor had drawn the shape of his liver across his stomach: it looked like the map of Africa. There were solemn warnings. He would have to knock off the grog for good.

"So why did he start drinking again?" I ask Maisie – my memory being that after eight or nine months they quarreled about something and he poured himself a whiskey to punish her. It would serve her right.

"Well, it was that big argument he had with you, wasn't it?" says Maisie.

"What about? I don't remember any argument."

"Who knows?" she says. "I think you were doing your honours at university."

*

A few years later, in 1974, my father had a massive cerebral haemorrhage. He and Maisie had gone – quite unusually, I think – for an afternoon walk together, and he felt this terrible pain in the back of his head. There was one of those inept funerals which Pakeha New Zealand has been so good at in the high, windy crematorium chapel above St Kilda beach. The vicar, who didn't know and probably disapproved of the departed, was like a bad actor trying out for Richard III, melodramatic and perfunctory by turns. I put the whole event out of mind as it went along. I tried not to pay attention. The RSA people did their thing with poppies; men from the ex-navalmen's association were pall-bearers, most of them looking as if they might go themselves at any minute. Jack was 63. One of the hymns was Tennyson's "Crossing the Bar", sometimes known as "The Sailor's Farewell":

Sunset and evening star,
    And one clear call for me!
And may there be no moaning of the bar
    When I put out to sea.

No moaning of the bar! As it happened, we were all going straight back there. There was a huge crush of bodies and noise. It was like a big, boisterous race day, or six o'clock closing, or the opening of the Oak Tree Inn. Maisie had decided to turn on free drinks, one of the few things she could be sure Jack would have wanted. His last shout, though this time he wouldn't be drinking. Who now would say, "Home, little bastards, home!" when everyone left at closing time? I had flown down from Wellington – for the time at the hospital, for the funeral. My brother Ian had come from London. Maisie was a widow. What would we all do now?

At one point one of the St Kilda's part-time barmen came up to me. He wasn't someone I knew. "Bad luck about your dad," he said. "There's never been much long-levity in our family either."

I shook his hand, and stared at him: he wasn't joking. In fact, he was offering consolation. He was pale, puffy, ginger, and alive.

I thought the usual thoughts. Then I said, "Cheers." Then I said, "Good health."

Be Drunk

Always you must make yourself drunk. That's it,
that's the thing. In order not to feel the terrible weight
of Time which breaks your back and bends you to the
earth, you must be continually drunk.

But on what? On wine, poetry, or virtue – as you like.
Just be drunk.

And if sometimes – on the steps of a palace, in the
green grass of a ditch, or in the bleak solitude of
your room – you wake, your drunkenness now going
or gone, then ask the wind, the wave, the star, the
bird, the clock – all that flies, all that wails and rolls
and sings, all that speaks – ask what the hour is . . .
and the wind, the wave, the star, the bird, the clock
will answer: "It is the hour to be drunk! And so,
not to be the martyred slave of Time, make yourself
drunk; be drunk without cease! On wine, on poetry,
on virtue – as you please."

– Baudelaire

Acknowledgements

Many thanks to Maisie Manhire, Bill Brien, Rona Barnett and Alister W. Macarthur.

I also found the following helpful:

Grog's Own Country: the Story of Liquor Licensing in New Zealand (2nd edition), by Conrad Bollinger, Auckland, 1967.

In the Same Room: Conversations with New Zealand Writers, eds Elizabeth Alley and Mark Williams, Auckland, 1992.

Mossburn: 100 Years Under the Dome, by V.G. Boyle, Invercargill, 1987.

Pubs Galore: History of Dunedin Hotels 1848-1984, by Frank Tod, Dunedin, 1984.

Pubs, Pints and People: 50 Years of the Invercargill Licensing Trust, by Clive A. Lind, Invercargill, 1994.

The Man on the Horse, by James K. Baxter, Dunedin, 1967.

The Story of Beer: Beer and Brewing – A New Zealand History, by Gordon McLauchlan, Auckland, 1994.

The Topdressers, by Janic Geelen, Te Awamutu, 1983.

New Zealand Licensee.